unlock your storybook heart

amanda lovelace

unlock
your
storybook
heart

amanda lovelace

Andrews McMeel
PUBLISHING®

books by amanda lovelace

the

series:

the princess saves herself in this one (#1)
the witch doesn't burn in this one (#2)
the mermaid's voice returns in this one (#3)

slay those dragons: a journal for writing your own story

believe in your own magic: a 45-card oracle deck & guidebook

***

the
things that h(a)unt
duology:

to make monsters out of girls (#1)
to drink coffee with a ghost (#2)

***

the
you are your own fairy tale
series:

break your glass slippers (#1)
shine your icy crown (#2)
unlock your storybook heart (#3)

***

flower crowns & fearsome things

for anyone who feels like
they've yet to find themselves:

i promise it's not too late.

contents

a note from the author

dearest reader, i'm so glad you've made it to the third & final collection in the "you are your own fairy tale" poetry trilogy! don't worry—you don't have to read *break your glass slippers* or *shine your icy crown* to understand this collection, though if you do end up enjoying it, then you may enjoy those collections, too. while these fictional stories are tied together by similar topics & themes, they ultimately have main characters & plots all their own. the one you hold in your hands currently, *unlock your storybook heart*, was loosely inspired by a few classic tales, most notably *beauty & the beast*, as well as a pinch of some of my own feelings & experiences.

thank you for letting me fill your heart with stories.

here's to many more to come.

laced with love,
amanda

let me tell you a bittersweet story

there is a girl
who has always been told
that she's one of the
quote-unquote *gifted ones*—

the kind who always sits
at the front of the class
& gets every question right.

"we just know you're going to
take the world by storm,"
they all tell her, proud as can be.

"what if i don't want to?"
she wishes she could say;
instead, she stays quiet
& smiles like a good girl.

let me tell you an even more bittersweet story

there is a girl
who can accomplish
just about anything
she puts her mind to—

even the things that
most people think
a girl can't *possibly* do.

even the things that
make her stress-cry,
tears clouding her glasses, but

she can't let herself down.
she can't let them down.
she can't let herself down.
she can't let them down.

part i

once there lived a locksmith who was so beloved that his tiny village crowned him king. this village was unlike any other. whenever a baby was born, which wasn't terribly often, the king bestowed upon each of them a gift: a one-of-a-kind key. after many tireless years, he & his wife—the queen—finally had a daughter of their own, & she was no exception to their sacred tradition. when he gently placed the key in her tiny fist, he said to her, "one day, this key will open the heart of your one true storybook love, & if it is indeed a true match, then their key, in turn, will also open yours . . ."

when she stumbles across a tome she likes, she lives & breathes it for days, weeks, & sometimes even months at a time. but before she begins her adventure, she always opens it up to the last page—carefully, never daring to crack its delicate spine—to ensure it has an ending filled with blissful tears, never devastated ones. you see, her life was not ripped straight out of a fairy tale; it has not always been very pretty, nor has it always been very predictable.

—this way, some part of it can be.

her books say

if you avoid all the stormy chapters,
how will you ever find meaning
in the rainbow-filled ones?

she's as beautiful as a classic poem
& she doesn't even need to try.

—*everyone except her can see that.*

her books say

did you know that mirrors were once seen as portals into fantastical realms? like most things, however, they lost much of their magic as humans became more & more concerned with the mundane & material aspects of living. you may look upon a reflective surface & see nothing but an ordinary girl, but there are great depths to you that you have yet to discover. next time, don't simply *look* at yourself & move along with your day; instead, stop to truly *see* yourself & note all the ways in which you are remarkable.

since she lost her mother at so young an age, she must now reach into the deepest chambers of her mind to conjure up even the smallest recollection of her. no corner ever goes unsearched. no curtain ever goes unmoved. no wardrobe ever goes unopened. when she *does* manage to catch the faint sound of her laugh or the barely-there scent of her strawberry shampoo, she clings to it for dear life, though she's usually convinced she's imagining it all.

—*she would do anything to spend a single moment with her again.*

her books say

from time to time, our minds can
have trouble differentiating between
a long-lost memory & a pleasant daydream.

so often, they feel exactly the same.

does the thought of it fill you with delight?
does it inspire you down to your bones?
does it bring you immense comfort?

then that's all that matters.

happy things aren't nearly common enough,
so feel no guilt as you grab hold of one
& put it on a shelf you can always see.

"clever & attractive?
that's certainly not allowed.

either you're hideous
underneath all of that makeup,

or you aren't nearly as intelligent
as you pretend to be."

—*a boy she didn't ask.*

her books say

no, you are not doomed to be the supporting character with a brave & bold line or two, existing solely to be the love interest in the man-hero's story. here's what they don't tell you: *you're just as interesting as he is.* maybe even more so, some would venture to say. despite what you've been led to believe, you can have beauty as well as a brain. you can have so much more than that, too. go on, keep confusing them. keep making them flustered by how *much* you are.

she will accept nothing less
than absolute perfection from herself.

—*she punishes herself more than anyone else does.*

her books say

it's valid to want the teetering stack of A's or the overflowing shelf of awards & trophies, but try to keep in mind that winning isn't supposed to be your everything, especially if you spend so much time focused on it that you miss the everyday enchantment all around you—the very first snowfall of the year, the ever-repeating numbers that follow you everywhere, & the goddess of a girl trying desperately to get even a crumb of your attention.

they say she's *wise beyond her years* like it's a rare & wonderful thing to behold, but she doesn't quite see it the same way. what they don't realize is that after everything she's had to endure, she didn't have a choice but to grow up quicker than she should have had to.

—& if she ever had a choice, things would be different.

her books say

some of the souls that are considered old
are actually just young & exhausted
due to the unfairness of the world
they did not have the means to prepare for.

he was not a man of many words,
but he made sure she knew that
she was, without a doubt, treasured.

she can only hope that he knows
he's a treasure to her, too.

—her father.

her books say

everyone expresses themselves a little differently. some people arc as quiet as a windchime caught in a gentle summer breeze, while some are as loud as a church bell on a sunday morning. the less grand expressions of love are in no way less valuable. in the steaming cups of tea served without request, in the photographs proudly displayed on desks, in the slippery paths salted for safety—*the signs are always there, should anyone ever try to go looking for them.*

no one had ever called her their *best friend*, had they?

—no; no, of course they had not.

her books say

would you allow your best friend
to talk down to herself
without trying to refute her?

no?

so don't do it to yourself,
either.

always respond to yourself
with the same amount of
respect, kindness, & pixie dust.

"father time is a sneaky, peculiar man. wasn't it only yesterday we were two little girls playing make-believe? i was a ship captainess drowning at sea & you, my siren queen, saved me at the very last moment, breathing life back into my lungs. in the years that followed, we drifted from each other as the waves did that imagined shore, as it so often goes with childhood friends. my most profound regret is that i wasn't brave enough to tell you, 'i think i like you.'"

—*journal entry no. 1.*

her books say

your story may seem like it has
far too many pages,

but by the time you're finished,
it will seem like far too few.

a good rule of thumb:

don't wait to do anything
you might not have a chance to do later,

& never, ever wait to tell someone
how you feel about them.

oh, her?

she's all self-deprecating jokes
with a hint of sarcasm,

so it's no wonder that
no one realizes how much pain

blooms just beneath
her perfectly placed cardigan.

—people are not always as they seem.

her books say

unfortunately, we live in a society that has a reputation for ignoring the suffering of their people out of sheer convenience. with any luck, it won't be that way much longer, but that's not where we are just yet. in the meantime, try never to lose sight of how utterly precious you are, because the world will keep on forgetting. you deserve to take a break. you are worthy of your own time, even if you're not being someone else's idea of *productive* or *useful*. you deserve to have fun, or to do nothing if that's what makes you happiest.

every time someone tells her she can't possibly accomplish what she sets out to do, she doesn't bother penning a response to them. she very well takes it to heart, not as something that discourages her, but as something that drives her forward— the ultimate challenge to prove herself, once & for all. she has no doubt that there will come a day when they'll have to eat their words. she *will* earn their praise.

—*ambitious is she.*

her books say

so many days will be spent feeling like
you're dancing underneath a thin glass
with every living soul watching,

so you spin & you twirl,
none of them caring if you grow weary.

it's almost as if every one of them
is wishing & waiting for you
to make a big enough mistake
so they can take it all away from you,

so you spin & you twirl,
living & dying for their approval,

when the truth of the matter is that
it's never been your responsibility
to keep them amused.

"why are you so serious?" they all ask her.

"because otherwise, who would
bother to take me seriously?" she replies.

—so-called resting bitch face.

her books say

one of the most outrageous fables ever told is that a girl's interests can only ever be silly & shallow. the idea has become so ingrained into the collective conscious that even girls believe this lie now, distancing themselves from anything that might make others perceive them as *just another vapid girl*. you need not sacrifice your authentic self to appease others, but some don't have the luxury of learning that until they're in their 20s, 30s, 40s, & beyond. promise us that if you should ever get lost along the way, you'll make your way back to whatever makes your heart sing magnificent melodies, & you'll embrace all of it, wholly unashamed.

whenever she puts on headphones, the whole world simply melts away, & she can ~~almost~~ feel the harps flowing into her veins to mend her sorrowful heart.

—*it's everything to her.*

her books say

it's a curious thing, isn't it,
how an artist can turn their hurt into
something so stunning that
it has the power to save strangers,
but it doesn't have the power
to save the artist themselves?

most people sleep to rest, but not her—
she sleeps to take off to someplace better.

—*her version of wonderland.*

her books say

when you slip down that rabbit hole
& enter your dreamworld,
you can do just about anything
that heart of yours desires—

you can go *anywhere* you want.
you can be *anyone* you wish.

the trick is to climb out of bed
& search for a way to
make a similar kind of magic
in your waking life,

for some say that dreams
are just the universe's way
of showing you
your highest potential.

& sunday nights were perhaps
the most excruciating of all
because it meant that monday
would be there shortly,

which meant that she would have to
withstand yet another week,
& that was *not* an easy thing to do.

eventually, even saturday nights were
spent barricaded in the bathroom
with the faucet on loud enough
to drown out the sound of her sobs,
for sunday would be there soon.

—*she doesn't know how much more she can take.*

we're well aware that the saying, "it won't always be like this," isn't the most helpful advice. even though it is a true statement, it's one that only unravels with much time & patience, & the waiting can be agonizing. you may not even notice the agony has subsided until you're at the crest of the mountain, looking down at the treacherous path below. but that moment will come, & when it does, i hope you'll stay to take in the wonder of the moonrise. i hope you'll send love down to the girl who never thought she'd make it so far.

when everyone in the house is fast asleep, she sneaks down into the kitchen, expertly stepping on the floorboards in such a way that they will not creak & wake anyone up. she's deprived herself for so long that food feels like an old & beloved friend she hasn't seen in ages, welcoming her in as their honored & cherished guest. they're the only one who can give her a sense of relief—the only one who truly understands her, until they no longer are. after she takes her final bite, they become her nemesis once more.

—*binge.*

her books say

who convinced you that you needed
to be this hard on yourself?

treat yourself with gentleness, lovely,
even when you feel like your life
is one big mess after another.

you're trying your very best
& you deserve *all* the credit for that.

she delays everything until
the very last possible minute—
even the things she likes to do.

she's afraid to even ask:

does that make her *lazy*?
does that make her *irresponsible*?

—*procrastination.*

her books say

not everything has to be done with a sense of urgency &
quickness. the hourglass is not running out, so you need not
act as though it is. take long, intentional sips of your coffee.
take small, intentional bites of your dinner. whatever you do,
don't judge yourself for taking all the time you need before
moving onto the next thing. everything in your day—no matter
how seemingly inconsequential—deserves to have its own
moment, even if it's just a few seconds to gather your thoughts
before you speak, for a girl saying the right words at the exact
right time could very well change lives.

it may not necessarily make *logical* sense to you, but there are certain things she must do in order to feel safe. before she leaves a room, she has to check & re-check every candlestick to make sure every wick has been properly extinguished. before she goes to bed, she has to check & re-check the knob to her front door to make sure it's tightly locked against intruders. there are times she runs far, far away with her worries. would anyone understand her preoccupations? would anyone be willing to take the time to see her for who she really is & decide they still want her?

—*the very idea seems unfathomable to her.*

her books say

don't settle for anyone who
accepts you in spite of
an integral part of yourself,

for that is *not* love.

don't stop looking until you
find someone who adores you
because of everything you are,

for that *is* love.

oh, how she wishes she had
someone who understands
exactly what she's going through.

oh, how she wishes she had
a mother she could confide in—

to offer her some sage advice,
to be her guide as she tries to
navigate these confusing woods.

—missing someone never gets easier, does it?

her books say

someday, science shall finally prove what we already know: *no one ever truly departs from this earth.* not when they take their last breath. not when they become cold to the touch. not when they're lowered into the soil. not even when their gravestone is overtaken by mushrooms & moss. know that when you speak aloud to them, they listen to every word; you need only trust what you hear back from the silence.

as the years go by, people ask her when she's finally going to stop being so "picky" & "persnickety" & find a nice man to settle down with. *why is it that they all assume i'm going to end up with a prince?* she wonders, perplexed.

—*don't presume you know what she wants.*

her books say

in this version of the age-old tale,
the beast is not a boy,

it is heteronormativity—

the spoken & unspoken expectation
that you will someday be
the princess to someone else's prince.

it doesn't have to be that way.

you could very well end up with
any person, royalty or not,
or perchance nobody at all.

you need only decide what's right for you.

her cat is always there for her,
even when nobody else bothers to be.

—*her soft companion.*

her books say

even the wisest among us will claim that cats are loathsome, soulless creatures, but that couldn't be further from the truth. cats can be fickle sometimes, sure, but when a cat trusts you enough to love you loudly? no poem could even begin to explain how amazing that feels.

"i'm not sure whether to consider it a dream or some kind of visitation, but either way, my mother was there with me once again. she took me in her arms & told me that i've been so focused on the brightness of my future that i forgot to plan for, well, just about everything else. i even forgot to plan for the most important thing of all—finding my passion. when she pulled away, the woman staring back at me was no longer my mother. it was me; *it was me all along.*"

—*journal entry no. 2.*

her books say

imagine this:

there could be a version of you
in every part of the future
who knows it will get better

because she's already
been through everything
you've been through
& managed to survive it all.

so, when you feel hopeless,
trust her resilience,
which is to say: *trust your own.*

disenchanted is she by the idea
of living her life the way
she thought it had to be.

—finally, she gets it.

her books say

you don't have to pick the big job in the big city if that's not what you want. it's okay to pick a calmer, quieter life. it's okay to pick the small seaside town where everyone knows a little too much about everybody else. it's okay to pick the job where you get to place your favorite books into eager hands all day long, only to go home & read all night long. no life is inherently more important than the other. the only thing that matters is that you pick the life that makes you excited to greet the morning sky each day.

& so the girl finally stopped reading the stories she thought she had to read because that's what everyone else seemed to be reading. she finally stopped watching television shows that no longer excited her, even if that's what everyone else made small talk about. she finally stopped wearing what was deemed *sensible* & *practical* & started wearing the clothes she was always afraid to wear instead, even if everyone else silently judged her when she passed by.

—*she's learning that it's okay to redefine herself.*

her books say

it would certainly be dull for you
to be the same as every other person,

but

it would be absolutely *tragic* for you
to be anyone except who you truly are.

these days, she makes the time to do all the things she once thought were a waste of time. today, she bakes chai muffins, enjoying the repetitive process that takes her mind off more serious things. when they're finished & the whole house smells like heaven on earth, she eats half of the tin, refocusing her mind when it wants to obsess about the numbers & the full-stomach guilt. instead, she fills her mind with good thoughts, like how nice & satisfied her belly feels after nourishing it, & how much she deserves to eat another for all the hard work that went into them.

—*the crumbs on her jeans are not a curse but a welcome sight.*

her books say

the tiniest steps are arguably
the most important,
so long as they're going in
the right direction,

but if you end up wandering
paths you've outgrown,
there's nothing to worry about.

finding your way is
something that takes practice,
& practicing means you're
bound to make some mistakes.

look at it this way:
at least you'll have wisdom to share.

she can admit that her creations
aren't always nice to look at—

far from it, actually,
but that doesn't really matter to her.

who cares about being *perfect*?
what's wrong with being *perfectly acceptable*?

—*the green-rose princess.*

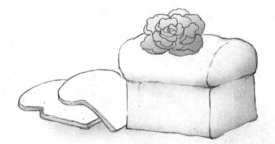

her books say

you can find immense pleasure in doing something yet not be
an expert at it, just as you can be a self-proclaimed fan of
something yet not know every microscopic detail about it.
believe it or not, your existence is not supposed to be this
impeccably manufactured experience. darling, it's *supposed* to be
chaotic & weird from time to time, because that's what makes
it uniquely & wonderfully *yours.*

she spent so long thinking
she doesn't deserve good things
that whenever something
oh-so-wonderful happens to her,

she still waits for someone to
come breezing in to tell her
there's been some kind of mistake
as they snatch it away.

—*she's working on it, okay?*

her books say

some change happens gradually, some change happens in the blink of an eye, & some change manages to do both at the same time. think about it in terms of how summer transforms into autumn: it seems like the leaves will never stop being green, will never stop dancing in the sunlight, until one morning you look out your window & every tree has been touched by midas. rest assured, your golden hour is coming. the more love & patience & compassion you give yourself, the closer you'll get. trust the process.

in the quietest corner of the library, she's all concentration with a dash of messy bun, as per usual, so she nearly misses the gorgeous girl with the sword & shield taking notice of her— *almost, but not quite.*

—*the knight.*

her books say

here's your chance, princess.
go on, let her sweep you off your feet.

when the clock strikes twelve & their lips meet for the first time in the soft glow of fairy lights, she suddenly understands why the first storyteller was compelled to pick up a quill & scrawl a fairy tale. the writers got so much wrong, didn't they, but this—this feeling of *magic*, this feeling of *certainty*—they got right in its entirety.

—*new year's eve.*

her books say

here's a little-known secret:

january 1st isn't the only
new beginning.

new beginnings can happen
at any given minute,
at any given second—

you need only say when.

she's well aware that *first loves*
are so rarely ever *only loves,*

but don't be mistaken:

that won't stop her from
giving this her all.

for now, they're happy,
& they'll be together as long
as that remains to be.

—*she hopes it's forever & ever.*

her books say

history has shown us a great many things, has it not? it has shown us that some people begin as friends & end up as lovers; it has also shown us that some people begin as lovers & end up as friends, & so on & so forth. no matter what happens, know this, dear one: relationships—romantic or otherwise—do not have to be long-lasting in order to be important, to hold castle-sized meaning.

she prefers her hair up & out of the way, but she can't help but to notice the way her love looks at her when she keeps it down, tangles & all, so needless to say, she's been wearing it down a lot lately.

—*not all the time, mind you, just . . . more often.*

her books say

when a relationship first begins, things are so new & sparkly that you can become consumed by it, forgetting to nurture yourself in the process. it's crucial to make time for others, but it's also crucial to spend time alone, to get to know who you are when you're not around them—yes, even if your fondness for them is so vast you don't know what to do with all of it. the strength of your relationship with yourself will, in turn, strengthen your relationship with them.

the only way she can explain it:

she's a dimly lit café
on an autumn afternoon,

while her love is a sunlit museum
on a summer morning.

—does that make sense?

her books say

some of the greatest writers have said that opposites attract & that's a valuable piece of wisdom, to an extent. be different enough that you challenge each other in refreshing & exhilarating ways, but don't be so unalike that you never seem to be on the same page about anything. so yes, be your unique selves, but don't forget to complement each other in the ways that are most important, too.

the princess feels safer with her knight than any other, so before they leave the room together, she asks her to check the candlesticks to make sure every wick has been properly extinguished. before they go to bed, she even asks her to check the knob to the front door to make sure it's been tightly locked against intruders. & you know what? her knight does all of it happily, for she only wants to ease her princess-love's mind, no matter the cost.

—they've got that unfathomably real type of love.

her books say

you'll find that some people are in fact
better than the storybook heroes & heroines
you stay up all night for, falling

head-over-heels for them over
the course of a few hundred pages—
the ones who seem to have
not even a single discernable flaw.

they're all the better *because* they have flaws,
because they ever-so-bravely
embrace their vulnerable humanness.

her love adores her even when she's being impossible.

—*who knew?*

her books say

it's not always going to be
this easy, effortless thing,

but it's not always going to be
all tears & sadness either.

you'll know you've found
a person who's worthwhile when

you don't feel the need to
pretend around them,

because they'll know when you are.
somehow, they'll always know.

"dear reader, she's not just the love of my life—*she's the best friend i've ever had.* when she's not feeling particularly brave, i encourage her to get back on her white horse to save the day, because i know she can do it. in turn, when i've lost sight of everyday enchantment, she encourages me to get out there with some mason jars so i can find some & bottle it up, because she knows i can do that, too."

—*journal entry no. 3.*

her books say

one day you were reading fairy tales,
& then your life became one.

it has been an honor to witness.

should you ever need us again,
just pick us up wherever you last left us,

for it is our sincere belief that

there exists no life so complete
that it couldn't use a sprinkle more magic.

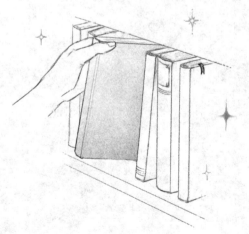

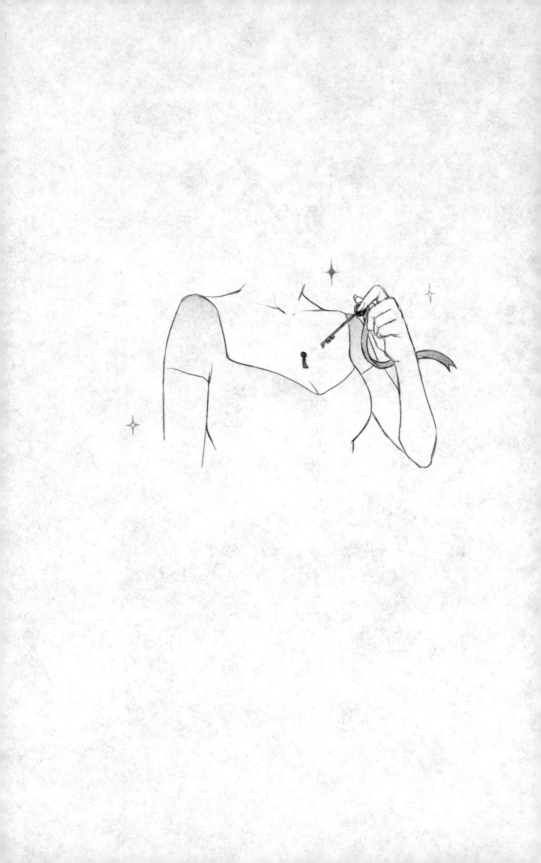

part ii

time unfurled so quickly that the young princess forgot all about the lock on her heart & the other person's key that would eventually unlock it. when she finally remembered, she pulled the key out from underneath her shirt, thinking to herself: *what if i can unlock my own heart with my own key?* soon after, she found out that was indeed the case after all, her heart unlocking effortlessly, for she had come such a long way on her journey of self-love & self-discovery. her most loyal knight was all smiles, completely unworried about their own promised happy ending, for she understood the enormous importance of being your own true love as well.

i wonder what my life would have been like if there had been girls like me in the fairy tales i read growing up—girls who fell for people regardless of their gender. perhaps if i had seen those feelings explained & explored on the page, i would have felt a little more understood. perhaps i would have had the confidence to embrace my true self earlier. alas, there's no way for me to go back in time & change it for the girl i was, but i can sure as hell read & write those tales in her honor now.

—*pink, yellow, blue.*

let no book collect dust.

you never know which one will
heal wounds you never knew you had.

no longer will i be the quiet girl who
softens her secretly-strong opinions
to avoid making people feel uneasy.

she may be as soft as a petal,
but she isn't as delicate as you think.

—treat her with equal parts care & caution.

i have a question: why is it that whenever a woman says she's a fan of something, a man immediately comes along to test the validity of it? actually, i think i already know the answer. so often, men choose to see women as brainless creatures, & if we happen to share the same interest, then it automatically challenges the complexity of it, & they no longer feel superior. they see us as a threat.

—*something to ponder.*

she isn't pretending to
like that novel
to get you to notice her.

she isn't pretending to
like that movie
to get you to notice her.

she isn't pretending to
like that comic
to get you to notice her.

she isn't pretending to
like that sport
to get you to notice her.

she isn't pretending to
like that game
to get you to notice her.

—she's just not that worried about impressing you.

actually, no, i *don't* take it as a compliment when you tell me how "hot" it is that i'm with a girl. believe it or not, my sexuality doesn't exist to add fuel to your fantasies.

—get far, far away from me & stay there.

she didn't give you a fake number
because she's trying to hurt your feelings.

she gave you a fake number
because that's what felt safest in the moment.

—*reflect upon why that is.*

this is me, lighting a candle in honor of every woman who sacrificed her own comfort & safety to make sure i was okay when it mattered most.

—*i wish you everything you could ever want.*

i see you doing incredible things.

i see you managing to
take care of yourself & everyone else,

even when no one says "thank you."
even when you're beyond exhausted.

i see all of it.

—*i'm endlessly in awe of you.*

pay no mind to that persistent voice in your head—the one that tells you that you're a failure for not going to college. *you are anything but a failure, you hear me?* if anything, you're a champion for choosing what's best for you, which won't always be what's best for everyone else. daring to walk the path less taken requires enormous courage.

—*i wish someone had told me this, so i'm telling you.*

intrusive & unpleasant thoughts
are merely just that—

thoughts.

imagine them as glitter in your palm
& blow them far, far away.

—a poem for you as much as it is for me.

think of your life like a first draft
that's forever in the works.

with the right words—
with the right editing—
it can *always* be improved upon.

—*nothing is so definitive that you need to decide it's doomed.*

i don't care if you're eight, twenty-eight, or eighty—embrace the unicorn that exists inside of you. it's never too late, so play like you're a child again. be loud. be silly. laugh as much as you possibly can. make the most of the time you get to be a human because there's nothing else that's quite as absurd & sad & wonderful all at the same time.

put the phone down.
no, not forever, just sometimes.

not because it's the root of
all your problems, like they claim,
but because it can make you
forget that you even *have* roots.

stop comparing your life to theirs.
stop endlessly doomscrolling.
stop giving away your energy.

even if just for a moment,
find your inner stillness.
feel mother earth
beneath your tired feet.

breathe in. breathe out.
let her restore your peace.

—as many times as you need.

i've stopped attempting to justify being kind-hearted to strangers by making up heartbreaking backstories for them, like maybe they're going through a nasty divorce or maybe their childhood dog just died or maybe their parents told them they're a disappointment or maybe they had a terrible week at work. i'm going to be kind-hearted no matter the circumstance, because isn't that the bare minimum treatment we all deserve from one another?

—*every day you determine the legacy you leave.*

i like to think of my body as an altar where i go to honor my goddess-soul, & just like any other goddess, i deserve daily offerings of food in exchange for the blessings i bestow upon this world. no more deprivation, only a deep sense of respect & admiration for myself.

—*i am devoted to my well-being.*

"this body has gained weight,
~~but~~ & this body is recovering."

"this body has gained weight,
~~but~~ & this body is beautiful."

—*midnight mirror musings.*

it's taken some time,
but i'm finally starting to
view my refrigerator as
the amazing thing it is.

its door leads me to the
most magical world
wherein i can be nourished,

which, in turn, gives me
the energy needed
to do so many things:

french braid my hair,
write long love letters,
collect rainwater,
& kiss pink-cloud-soft lips.

—*& that's just the beginning.*

if there's one lesson you should choose to take away from my story, then let it be this: *life is not something that can be experienced on a deadline.* sometimes you must completely let go—no expectations, no pre-conceived notions. *do* try to have faith that you'll end up someplace remarkable, no matter how many unusual characters you happen upon or tricky plot twists that unfold along the way.

—breaking the fourth wall.

what would my life have been like
if i had been encouraged to follow my heart
instead of following a paycheck?

—*i don't know, but i'm determined to find out.*

i believe everyone has a purpose, but i also believe that not everybody has a purpose so dramatic it could be made into a series of epic books that's eventually adapted into a series of epic blockbusters. sometimes just *living* is enough. sometimes just *feeling* is enough.

—*let it be enough.*

i. make a stranger's day.
ii. brew the perfect cup of coffee.
iii. witness a moonbow.
iv. have a bird land on my finger.
v. follow my every whim.

—*a list of things i want to experience before i die.*

you truly don't have to wait until a special occasion to do anything, so go on & put the holiday tree up in august. stay up till dawn making that instagram-worthy cake. wear those glistening green heels. sprinkle cinnamon on absolutely everything. & before you can make excuses—who cares what other people may think or say?

—*it's time you embraced what gives you joy.*

i didn't think i could ever finish writing a book, & then i did it. i didn't think i could ever paint anything worth hanging on a wall where others could see, & then i did it. i didn't think i could ever buy a plant & keep it alive for more than a few days, & then i did it. once i consciously stopped letting self-doubt rule every aspect of my life, i learned it was the only thing that was ever truly standing in my way.

—*nothing & no one else.*

what's that one thing you would do for yourself
if only you could muster up the confidence?

_____

_____

_____

—now go do it anyway.

no relationship should make you feel drained or frightened at every turn.

—it should make you feel strong enough to break fairytale curses.

it may be hard to believe sometimes,
but there is someone out there
who will love you enough to stay after
the pen writes the words *the end*—

when those wild & passionate nights
inevitably transform into
those quiet & peaceful evenings.

the right one will turn to you & say,
"let's write the sequel, darling."

—even if that person is you.

hey, you. yes, you. *the very person reading this right now.* you deserve a happiness brighter than every firefly in the entire world lit up at the exact same time.

—*your forever reminder.*

being in a relationship does not
make me any less independent.

being in a relationship does not
make me any less of a badass.

—*i can be whatever the hell i want to be.*

before you, no one bothered to remember how i take my tea, but you get it right every time. when i try to make it now, it never tastes as good as yours.

—*it's the little things, sometimes.*

when i can't sleep because i keep getting
caught up in the *worst-case* scenarios,

she reminds me that the *best-case* scenarios
are more than possible, too,

but it ultimately doesn't matter because
she'll be there through all of it.

i hogged the blankets at night, so she eventually wove one big enough for both of us. the cabinets & shelves overflowed with my collection of teacups, so she built more without question. i was sad that i didn't have a mother to share my daily anecdotes with, so she said, "that's okay, because you'll get to call mine 'mom' one day."

—*swoon.*

thank you, darling, for never
making me feel like an inconvenience,

for always allowing my branches to
grow in all sorts of directions,
even if they bend at awkward angles.

may yours keep growing, too.

may our branches get so tangled
that we eventually grow together
as the trees sometimes do,

wrapping around each other
for all eternity.

—i imagine we'd make the whole forest jealous.

if you were to leave me, i know i'd eventually be alright. i've already survived so much, so i know i could survive you running through the castle we built together only to keep going until you reach our front gate, locking it behind you before you leave for the final time.

—*just because i'd be okay doesn't mean i ever want that to happen.*

i can't wait to count gray hairs with you.
i can't wait to do everything there is to do.
i can't wait to see everything we'll see.
i can't wait to meet all the people we'll be.

—as cliché as it is, it must be said.

i have no doubt that
we were together in other lives.

we may have been glass slippers
from the same pair—

we may have been ice-like crystals
on the same crown—

we may have been antique keys
stored in the same box—

& now we finally get to be lovers
sitting on the same small garden bench.

—*we will always find each other again.*

i'm a believer & she has a reputation for being a skeptic, but she still asks me to tuck lavender inside of her pillow so she can have a peaceful night's rest.

—*i guess some people can make you believe anything is possible.*

i refuse to kiss you like it's the last time,
because there will never *be* a last time.

—they'll find our ghosts kissing everywhere.

on any given day, i imagine a thousand scenarios in which you &
my mother are alive at the very same time. *what would she think
of you?* i can't help but to wonder. *would she like you?* & then i feel
a little ridiculous, because of course she would like you. how
could she not? she would adore anyone that makes me feel as
cozy-at-home-in-a-woodland-cottage as you do.

when you've already lost a parent, it's not easy to watch the living one age. i try never to take our time for granted, but what i've sometimes failed to realize is that living in fear of what the future will bring *is* a way of taking our time for granted, albeit unintentionally. i try to remember that i'm a being of the here & now—not the future days, & sure as hell not the ones of the past. i need to live *here*, within every single delicate moment we've been so graciously gifted.

—*that's what i try to do, even if i'm imperfect at it.*

i have to trust that the gods
& the goddesses are real.

i have to trust that charging
a crystal with intention
will bring me peace & protection.

i have to trust that i'll die & wake
in a land of everlasting summer
& embrace my loved ones again
in the glittering-sun glen.

—some days, that trust is all that keeps me together.

i miss you like...

~~a book misses its shelf.~~
~~a potion misses its bottle.~~
~~a fox misses the woods.~~
~~a witch misses their hat.~~

a daughter misses her mother.

—no simile can capture the pain.

i know losing someone can make you feel like you're nothing but a chipped wineglass with a forever-missing piece, but the thing is, a wineglass with a forever-missing piece doesn't need to be thrown into the garbage. the rest of the glass is still whole. you can still drink from it—you just need to learn to be mindful of the parts that can hurt you.

i like to think that
you're one of my spirit guides

leading me not to follow
in the direction of your footsteps,

but leading me to a clearing
where i can leave some of my own.

"nowadays, i never have a chance to grieve you for too long because you always seem to show up somewhere. i saw a cardinal the other day, & i know it must have been you because you always acted so wonderstruck by their bright red feathers against the backdrop of evergreens. these little reminders comfort me for so many reasons, but lately, they've been giving me the chance to become still & take in all the lovely things i may be missing out on. thank you for that. i promise never to miss out on my life again."

—*the final journal entry.*

part iii

& so the green-rose princess & her loyal knight lived happily ever after, not just because they had each other, but because they had themselves. eventually, they decided they would settle in the tiny village in which they were raised & that they adored so much. after the princess's father died of old age, they took the time to weep before they stepped up to rule respectively as queen & queen. they ended up building a castle of their own, where only love could thrive—a place where every single person was happy & taken care of. it was more beautiful than any fairy tale that had been written.

special acknowledgments

i. *my spouse, parker lee*—thank you for encouraging me every step of the way & for making me chai lattes to help me survive my long writing days!

ii. *janaina medeiros*—thank you for the illustrations that bring my words to life in the most magnificent manner.

iii. *christine day & mira kennedy*—thank you for your crucial feedback—the compliments as well as the critiques—on every single collection, this one included!

iv. *my friends & family*—thank you for always keeping my cup filled with love & support.

v. *my readers*—thank you for giving me so many reasons to keep writing.

about the author

amanda lovelace (she/they) is the author of several bestselling poetry titles, including her "women are some kind of magic" series as well as her "you are your own fairy tale" trilogy. she is also the co-creator of the *believe in your own magic* oracle deck. when she isn't reading, writing, or drinking a much-needed cup of coffee, you can find her casting spells from her home in a (very) small town on the jersey shore, where she resides with her poet-spouse & their three cats.

follow the author

 @ladybookmad

 @ladybookmad

 amandalovelace.com

Andrews McMeel Publishing
a division of Andrews McMeel Universal
1130 Walnut Street, Kansas City, Missouri 64106

www.andrewsmcmeel.com

22 23 24 25 26 RR2 10 9 8 7 6 5 4 3 2 1

ISBN: 978-1-5248-5195-8

Library of Congress Control Number: 2021948674

Illustrations by Janaina Medeiros

Editor: Patty Rice
Art Director/Designer: Julie Barnes
Production Editor: Dave Shaw
Production Manager: Cliff Koehler